MW00440125

what's being said

The Oy Way is a great way for newcomers to Yiddish, as well as those who have spoken it for decades, to enjoy the pleasures of this mama loshen *(mother tongue) in a most enjoyable and different way.*

Eugene Driker
Chair, Yiddish Book Center

Humor research has concluded that 20 seconds of hearty laughter is equivalent to 20 minutes on a rowing machine. With The Oy Way, *you can enjoy both simultaneously.*

Paul Krassner
Author and satirist

Should be more than a hoot and enlightening to many.

Chungliang Al Huang
Founder-president, Living Tao Foundation;
author or co-author of a dozen books
about Tai Ji and Eastern philosophy

It works! After reading only a few pages of The Oy Way *and following the easy-to-understand instructions, I laughed so hard that I could say* gey avek *to all my mental and physical pain. I love the photos too.*

Judith A. Sokoloff
Editor, *Na'Amat USA Woman* magazine

Sure to be a hit with Judeo-yoginis and spiritual fitness buffs of all faiths and persuasions.

Stephen Kessler
Author of *Tell It to the Rabbis* and *The Tolstoy of the Zulus*

*The Oy Way combines some form of physical relaxation
therapy with Yiddish vocabulary and phrases. Partly in jest,
partly seriously, the author describes movements
and exercises that are meant to lead a person down the
"path of most resistance." So if you're looking for something
entertaining, therapeutic, and Yiddish-related,
this might be the book for you.*

Shaul Seidler-Feller
Co-creator of Yiddish Word-of-the-Week

This is going to be an excellent book to give as a present.

Jay Coleman
Writer, editor, founder of Coleman Communications

Lessons from the Oy Way Master himself.

Dave Mora
Novelist, editor, co-founder of Core Fitness Company

I love it! Can't get over the humor!

Peter Garrone
Artist and writer, New Jersey

*If I never get through the actual gestures . . . I will exercise
my stomach muscles through stress-relieving laughter.*

Tim Mitchell
Art director, graphic design lecturer,
San Jose State University

*The Oy Way great idea. Lets you know how to put your
Yiddish into action.*

Katherine Forrest, MD
Co-founder, The Commonweal Institute

also by Harvey Gotliffe

Awareness in Advertising

Highway 17 Almanack & Gazetteer

My Father Was Born on Trafalgar Street

The Ben & Zen, Now and Then Writing Almanack

*Responsible and Ethical Decision Making:
Advertising and Editorial Content*

THE OY WAY

*Following the path
of most resistance*

Harvey Gotliffe

Cogitator Publications · 2012

Published and distributed by
Cogitator Publications
P.O. Box 3602
Santa Cruz, CA 95063

The Oy Way movements are designed to give you a joyful, gentle and positive experience, regardless of your age, gender, or physical condition. The author and publisher disclaim any and all liability arising directly or indirectly from the use of any information contained in this book. Please feel free to consult your health care provider before trying any of these movements.

Photography by Amy Gotliffe

Book design by Stephen Pollard
Set in ITC Legacy and Serifa

ISBN 978-1-882302-36-9

Printed in the United States of America

Library of Congress Control Number: 2011962839

contents

introduction

When Yiddish was brought to America by Eastern European Jewish immigrants in the late nineteenth and early twentieth centuries, the vulnerable language could have languished and died.

But today, Yiddish is very much alive, and has become a venerable part of our conversation; it appears in our music, movies, media and dictionaries.

A politician deriding President Obama said he had a lot of *chutzpah,* and a national bank's advertising headline read "1.35% APY vs. *Bupkus.*" *New York Times* columnist David Brooks wrote that he found a *heymish* place while on a trip to Africa.

A crossword puzzle's answer to the clue "Jewish dough" was *gelt,* and a *Huffington Post* headline implored readers to "Quit *Kvetching* and Do Something."

In an increasingly hurried, harried, and hectic electronic world, simple Yiddish expressions offer profound wisdom, and have helped provide physical, emotional, and mental stress relief to true believers. Individuals became their own sages, and have survived and even prospered by inculcating these expressions into their daily lives, reconfiguring them into prophetic sayings.

The Oy Way offers a *meshuge* philosophy that combines meditation, exercise and humor, set forth in easy-to-learn Yiddish. It will be a *mekhaye* to read and follow—even if it's just a *bisl* at a time.

However, *shlepn* children or grandchildren to after-school activities is not a beneficial form of exercise. Being *in mitn drinen* a crisis at work doesn't help to lower stress, especially when there may be too much *shrayen.* Someone seeking an escape from stress can't lower cholesterol by nervously *nashn* fat-laden foods.

The Yiddish found in *The Oy Way* blends a rhythmic, flowing form of moving meditation with a unique way of thinking.

At times, these expressions introduce turmoil in the midst of tranquility, and then impose humor into the resultant chaos and disorder. This form does not guarantee inner peace, but knowing that others may be sharing the sar resultant agony brings solace to some. The true believer can inadvertently be led on a journey down the path of most resistance.

It is a special journey everyone can follow, even if your mind is closed, as long as your heart is open.

It is *The Oy Way*.

P.S. If you don't *farshteyn* a word, turn to the Glossary and *lernen*.

For links to useful Yiddish sites, access **Yiddish Links** at

www.theoyway.com

where information can also be found
about purchasing additional copies of this book.

---

acknowledgments

With their unbending devotion to preserving the Yiddish language and culture, I thank members of the Silicon Valley Holocaust Survivors Association, who have inspired me to try to do the same.

I have learned about the importance of doing movements to help maintain and improve physical and mental health through my Tai Ji mentor, Chungliang Al Huang, founder of The Living Tao Foundation.

Philip "Fishl" Kutner, the publisher of *Der Bay,* has done his utmost to connect me to the world of Yiddish, and I am grateful for his consistent encouragement and help in preparing this book.

I was fortunate to have Stephen Pollard as my book designer and editor; his insightful suggestions have helped to make *The Oy Way* what it is.

My daughter, Amy Beth Gotliffe, is the book's photographer extraordinaire. Her continual encouragement was a needed ingredient to complete the book.

My wife, Carmen Sarah Gotliffe, was always there to support and encourage me. She helped me to stay focused, and ensured that I never drifted from my goal of completion.

I am grateful to all the relatives, friends and fellow authors who nudged me to go on.

All the aforementioned people made it possible to help dissipate much of the *oy vey* in my life, and allowed me to finish writing and publishing *The Oy Way.*

the story of Yiddish

prelude

Once upon a time, nearly a thousand years ago, there were people with no country of their own. From the eleventh through the fifteenth centuries, they were expelled from whatever European land they had settled. At times, they were unable to take all of their physical possessions with them. However they always took what was most important—their religious beliefs and their language. The people were Jews, their religion was Judaism, and their language was Yiddish.

when Yiddish began

In the tenth century, Jews from France and Italy migrated to the German Rhine Valley, and began speaking Yiddish in an Ashkenazi culture. The name came from the medieval Hebrew designation for the territory; Ashkenazim or Ashkenazi Jews were literally "German Jews."

The term "Yiddish" comes from the German word for Jewish—*jüdisch*—and to Germans a Jew was *ein Yid*. Yiddish developed as a blend of German dialects with Hebrew, Aramaic, Slavic languages and traces of Romance languages. It was the *lingua franca* of Ashkenazi Jews.

By the late 1200s, Jews had created a language rooted in Jewish history that they used in their daily lives and in business among themselves. When they did business with Gentiles, Jews spoke the language of their countrymen.

Today in the United States, you could be greeted in New Orleans with "How y'all?" or in Brooklyn with a thickly accented "New Yawk" hello.

In earlier times, Yiddish evolved into four accents or dialects, also depending on the locale. There was Eastern and Western Yiddish, and Eastern Yiddish encompassed three distinct dialects. A *Litvak* spoke Lithuanian Yiddish and lived in either Lithuania, Belarus or northeastern Poland. A *Galitzyaner* spoke Polish Yiddish and resided in Poland and the Austro-Hungarian province of Galicia. Those who spoke Ukrainian Yiddish were from the Ukraine, Romania, southeastern Poland and eastern Galicia. Western European Yiddish was closer to German, and began to decline in the eighteenth century.

Hebrew was the language of *davnen*—praying—used in ritual and religion. It became known as the *loshn koydesh*, the sacred language used exclusively by men. In the Ashkenazi community, women weren't considered holy enough for Hebrew, but they learned to read and write in Yiddish—the *mame loshn*—the mother tongue. Men were able to read both.

the movement eastward

Jews have always been a target for persecution, expulsion and annihilation. In 1095, Pope Urban II called for the first crusade to seize the Holy Land from Muslim infidels. As crusaders marched through Germany, they sought out "infidel" Jews and offered them the choice of death or conversion to Christianity. Thousands of Jews were slaughtered when they refused to abandon their faith.

After the Crusades, many Ashkenazi Jews migrated eastward, forming communities in non-German-speaking areas, including Hungary, Poland, Belarus, Lithuania, Russia, Ukraine, and elsewhere. Jews were forced out of France in 1182, twice in the fourteenth century, and out of England in 1290.

The oldest surviving literary document in Yiddish is a blessing in a Hebrew prayer book from 1272. The 1526 Prague Passover *Haggadah* contained the first page printed in Yiddish. The advent of the printing press resulted in an increase in the amount of Yiddish material produced.

In the thirteenth century, Yiddish replaced both Hebrew and local languages in conversation. In the fourteenth and fifteenth centuries, songs and poems were written in Yiddish, using letters of the Hebrew alphabet. During that time, Jews were expelled from Hungary, Lithuania, Germany twice, Austria, Spain and Portugal.

The Jewish population moved further eastward into Poland and Russia and in the late Middle Ages, Slavic elements were incorporated into Yiddish. Jews further developed the language and included elements of Hebrew, French, Italian, and various German dialects.

In the fifteenth century, Europe's largest Jewish communities were in Poland, and remained the heart of Ashkenazi Jewry until their demise in the Holocaust. From the fifteenth through the nineteenth centuries, Eastern European Jews lived in *shtetls*—small towns—and in large cities.

In 1792, Catherine the Great created a "Pale of Settlement" in Russia where Jews were forced to live in their *shtetls* within its boundaries—boundaries they were not allowed to cross without a special pass. The Pale covered western Russia, Belarus, Lithuania, Poland, Ukraine, Romania and eastern Hungary.

By the eighteenth century, the Yiddish language was between 10% and 20% Hebrew and Aramaic, and nearly 75% Germanic. Romance words and Slavic words made up the rest.

the people's language

During the late nineteenth and early twentieth centuries, secular Yiddish literature flourished; much of its original growth was attributed to the writing of three major authors. The grandfather of Yiddish literature was Sholem Abramovich (1835–1917), who wrote under the name Mendele Mocher Sforim. Isaac Leib Peretz (1852–1915), better known as I. L. Peretz, was a writer of social criticism, plays and short stories. Solomon Rabinovich (1859–1916) was a Yiddish author and playwright who wrote under the name Sholem Aleichem. His stories about Tevye the dairyman were the basis for *Fiddler on the Roof.*

In the 1897 and 1917 census, more than 95% of Russian Jews listed Yiddish as their native tongue, and for many it was their only language. Jews were subjected to frequent pogroms—terrifying acts of destruction. The increase in their usage and severity ordered by tsarist edicts between 1877 and 1917 caused further fear.

Between 1870 and 1914, some two million Eastern European Jews came to America. They had the foresight and the *mazl* to escape the upcoming rampant waves of anti-Semitism in Europe. Many brought little more than their Yiddish language with them, and the majority who settled in New York considered Yiddish their native language.

Jews, who had been known as "the people of the book," became the people of the press. The first Yiddish-language newspaper was published in New York in 1870, and in 1875 the *Jüdisches Tageblatt* (Jewish Daily News) was the first Yiddish daily to survive. Its circulation reached 100,000 by 1900, but it was challenged by the *Forverts* (The Jewish Daily Forward), whose circulation peaked at 250,000 in 1929. The *Forverts* helped to Americanize immigrants by offering a popular *Bintel Brief* advice column, a variety of human interest stories, and highbrow and lowbrow literature.

By 1914 there were ten Yiddish daily newspapers, with a combined circulation of more than 750,000. Political parties and interest groups across the spectrum started their own papers, including the socialists, communists, centrists, labor workers and Orthodox Jews.

Polish-born Isaac Bashevis Singer (1901–1991) was a journalist and columnist for the *Forverts* from the 1930s into the 1960s. He was also a leading figure in Yiddish literature, writing short stories and novels first in Yiddish, then translating them into English. In 1978, Singer was awarded the Nobel Prize in Literature.

During the 1920s, Yiddish was emerging as a major Eastern European language. Its rich literature was widely published, Yiddish theater and Yiddish film prospered, and it even achieved status as one of the official languages of both the Belarusian and Galician Soviet Socialist Republics. In 1925, YIVO was founded in Wilno, Poland, now Vilnius, Lithuania, as the *Yidisher Visnshaftlekher Institut,* the Yiddish Scientific Institute. It was the preeminent repository and publisher of Yiddish-language materials.

In Poland's 1931 population of about 32 million, nearly one in ten were Jewish, and more than 87% of them spoke Yiddish. In 1937, there were 150 Yiddish newspapers and journals, with a combined circulation of more than 500,000.

almost its demise

The US Immigration Act of 1924 prevented large numbers of Eastern European Jews and others from coming to America. In May 1939, Great Britain produced a white paper that restricted Jewish migrations to Palestine to 75,000 in the coming four-year period. The actions of both governments helped to bring about the decimation of Europe's Yiddish-speaking Jewish population by the Nazis. The Act also eliminated a vital source of new readers and the Yiddish press circulation in America began to decline. Children of immigrants actively strove for cultural assimilation, and they were more likely to read an English-language newspaper than the Yiddish *Forverts.*

Before the Nazis invaded Poland in September 1939, there were more than nine million Jews in Europe. In Russia, Romania, Lithuania and Latvia, there were a combined total of 7.3 million Jews, and almost 75% of them spoke Yiddish.

Nearly six million Jews were slaughtered during the Nazi era, of which two-thirds were Yiddish speakers. A Lithuanian rabbi in Kovno, Lithuania wrote that "the bandit Hitler" not only killed a people, but also tried to kill a culture and a language. The Nazis destroyed schools, *shuls,* books, Yiddish theaters, movies, and radio programs, and the Holocaust led to a dramatic decline in the use of Yiddish.

Millions of Yiddish speakers survived the war, including those living in America, yet further assimilation in the United States and the Soviet Union diminished the daily use of Yiddish. In Russia, Stalin was suspicious of Jews and their "secret language," and Yiddish culture became a prime target. Jewish institutions were suppressed and its leaders, actors, writers and poets were arrested. In August 1952, thirteen prominent Yiddish writers were executed.

Yiddish barely survives

Yiddish-speaking Holocaust survivors sought refuge in places relatively free from anti-Semitism, including the United States, and Israel, which seemed to be a promised land for Yiddish speakers. Unfortunately, its leaders feared that if the seeds of Yiddish were allowed to be planted, then both the country's new identity as a special haven for Jews and its *lingua franca*, Hebrew, might not flourish. Those in power surpressed a nascent Yiddish theater that had been created by survivors as a dedication to and a remembrance of the way things were. It was a *shande*—a shame—but an understandable one for a new nation.

Then and now, Yiddish was spoken on a daily basis, primarily in Jerusalem's religious neighborhoods. A tale is told about an American grandmother visiting Israel who was overheard on a bus teaching her ten-year-old grandson a few words in Yiddish. A man sitting across the aisle said, "Tell me why you are teaching your grandson Yiddish. You know that Israel's national language is Hebrew." She looked at the man and said, "Because I want him to remember he's a Jew." Until Israel was established in 1948, Jews were a people without a country, a government, or a military, and their Yiddish language was one fragile connection between them.

After World War II, Jews in the United States sought to be assimilated. They encouraged their children to become even more American, and in doing so, discouraged them from learning Yiddish.

Yiddish-speaking Holocaust survivors also wanted their children to have a better opportunity to become successful, and they equated success with becoming more Americanized by speaking "perfect" English. With Yiddish slowly being silenced, the old country and its rich culture were becoming a fading memory.

Parents of baby boomers viewed Yiddish as the old-fashioned language of their parents and grandparents. By 1960, only 3% of American children enrolled in Jewish education learned Yiddish. At the same time, Yiddish newspaper circulation continued to decrease.

In 1999, the Minority Language Committee of Sweden formally declared Yiddish as one of its country's five minority languages. In its latest *Atlas of the World's Languages*, UNESCO, the United Nations World Heritage organization, referred to Yiddish as a "definitely endangered" language. That foreboding term means "children no longer learn the language as mother tongue in the home." What would become of the *mame loshn* if it were no longer the mother tongue?

The US Census Bureau's 2007 survey of language use revealed that only 158,991 people spoke Yiddish at home, and that figure had declined in every census since 1980. The major exception is found in the more closely knit, ultra-Orthodox (Hasidic) communities, but even many modern Orthodox Jews do not know Yiddish. However, there has been a resurgence in Yiddish learning and language, with many Jews embracing *Yiddishkeyt*.

Yiddish in America

Yiddishkeyt reflects a person's "Jewishness." It is an eclectic mishmash of mannerisms, speech, and a cultural and emotional connectivity to things Jewish. It could involve attending Jewish movies and plays; enjoying Jewish humor, books, periodicals, and music; and associating with and supporting Jewish organizations. You don't have to speak Yiddish to be part of *Yiddishkeyt*, but if you are of Ashkenazi descent, it helps.

When Yiddish theater was banned in Russia in 1883, some of its troupes first went to London and then came to New York. Today, Yiddish theater is doing well in New York; the National Yiddish Theater *Folksbiene* produces both Yiddish plays; and plays from other languages translated into Yiddish. The *Folksbiene* began in 1915 when there were fifteen Yiddish theater companies in New York alone, and others throughout the world.

Between 1936 and 1939, The Golden Age of Yiddish Film, seventeen Yiddish sound films were produced in the United States, and many reflected the immigrant experience in America. The National Center for Jewish Film at Brandeis University has restored thirty-eight Yiddish feature films, and some are shown at international film festivals.

If you want to *lernen a bisl* Yiddish today, you can do so in a university classroom, a *shul*, Jewish community centers, in small study groups, on your own, or online. The academic study of Yiddish received a boost in 1949 with the publishing of Uriel Weinreich's *College Yiddish: An Introduction to the Yiddish Language and to Jewish Life and Culture.*

Yiddish is taught in universities across the United States, and a graduate program in Yiddish Studies at Columbia University began in 1952 under Weinreich's leadership. Oxford University offers an MSt (Master of Studies), and there are intensive summer study programs offered in the United States, Canada, Israel, Poland, Lithuania and Germany.

There are also classes available on line from the Yiddish Book Center, founded in 1980 by Aaron Lansky. The Center has helped rescue more than a million Yiddish volumes and has diligently worked to preserve the Yiddish language. Since 1998, it has digitized the full texts of more than eleven thousand Yiddish books, and they can be downloaded at no charge. The Center has helped establish Yiddish collections at the Library of Congress, the British Library, and more than 600 libraries around the world, including national libraries in Australia, China and Japan. In 2010, a Yiddish-Japanese dictionary was published.

In 1981, the Yiddish Book Center began publishing *Pakn Treger*—the Book Peddler. It is written in English, with some Yiddish, and looks at contemporary Jewish life and its Yiddish roots. In 1983, the Yiddish-language *Forverts* became a weekly newspaper, and now has a circulation of 5,000. In 1990 the *Forward* began as the English-language weekly version, and its circulation has grown to 26,000. The *Forward* went online in 1998, followed by the *Forverts*, which tries to reach a younger, worldwide audience of Yiddish speakers.

Today, there are Yiddish-language newspapers, magazines, as well as Yiddish radio programming, with one station each in Boston and New York, and others around the world.

Highly spirited klezmer music began in the Hasidic culture of Eastern Europe in the 1700s. The name comes from the Hebrew words *klei* and *zemer*, and literally means "vessels of song." It was played at joyful celebrations such as weddings, and that tradition continues in America, where its melodic and soulful sounds have helped spur interest in all things Yiddish. There are more than two hundred klezmer groups found in thirty-six states.

Yiddish melodies were sung and played by many artists, including the Andrews Sisters recording *"Bei Mir Bist Du Schön"* in 1937, Cab Calloway's *"Utt Da Zay"* in 1939, and Billie Holiday's rendition of *"My Yiddishe Momma"* in 1956.

Many organizations in the United States and around the world work to preserve and promulgate Yiddish. In its world headquarters in New York, YIVO's library has more than 385,000 volumes, and its archives contain more than 24 million pieces, including manuscripts, documents, and photographs. YIVO offers cultural events and films, adult education, Yiddish language classes, and a six-week intensive summer program.

The Workmen's Circle/Arbeter Ring is a Yiddish language-oriented, American Jewish fraternal organization committed to social justice, the Jewish community, and Ashkenazic culture. To perpetuate the Yiddish language and culture, its extensive online Jewish Book Center offers songbooks, CDs, klezmer CDs, textbooks, instruction books, and dictionaries, as well as books of Yiddish literature.

The International Association of Yiddish Clubs helps unify Yiddish activities and events, holds international conferences, and strives to keep the Yiddish language, literature and culture alive.

Yiddish lives on

The Yiddish language has survived centuries of fervent anti-Semitism, pogroms in Eastern Europe, and atrocities committed by the Nazis. But the Third Reich was destroyed, while the remnants of European Jews and their coveted Yiddish language still survive. Today, many Holocaust survivors relish conversing in Yiddish whenever and wherever they get together.

On December 8, 1978, Isaac Bashevis Singer received the Nobel Prize in Literature and delivered his acceptance lecture in both Yiddish and English. He concluded by saying, "Yiddish has not yet said its last word. It contains treasures that have not been revealed to the eyes of the world. It was the tongue of martyrs and saints, of dreamers and cabalists—rich in humor and in memories that mankind may never forget. In a figurative way, Yiddish is the wise and humble language of us all, the idiom of the frightened and hopeful humanity."

The vulnerable Yiddish language could have languished and died, but instead it has become a venerable part of our society. The thousand-year-old story of Yiddish is not over. It may not be as richly told as before, but it would be a mistake to write it off. Now is the time to continue writing the current chapter, which begins "Once upon a time in the twenty-first century."

why THE OY WAY

Growing up in Detroit in the 1950s, some of us had family members who came from Europe and spoke Yiddish in their homes. They kept their conversations private, so we understood only a *bisl* of what they said.

In 1982, the year after both my parents died seven weeks apart, I decided to travel to places where their parents had lived. My father's parents, Max and Annie Gotliffe, were born in 1876 in what is now Lithuania, and I was determined to go there.

I bought *Lithuanian Self-Taught*; I then discovered that there was a small Jewish community comprised primarily of Holocaust survivors. At Borenstein's Book Store in Detroit I also purchased *Say It in Yiddish,* a pocket-sized 182-page phrase book for travelers. It contained a mélange of useful and useless phrases, some of which I planned to memorize, but never found the time to do so.

I flew to Paris, then visited Scandinavia and parts of Russia, before arriving in Vilnius, Lithuania in June. My first Friday night there was my father Henry's *yortzayt* and I cautiously entered the Choral Synagogue on Pylimo Street. Its musty odor reminded me of the small *shul* in Detroit where I had my *bar mitzvah*.

There were a dozen or so congregants in their seventies standing in front near the *bime*. I tried to be inconspicuous and slipped into a seat in the last row. The ten or so regulars eyed me, then three of them approached me, while the rest hovered a few steps behind.

I was only able to blurt out *"Bist a Yid* from America." Suddenly I was overwhelmed by their questions in Yiddish. Although I had the phrase book, I was unable to look up answers, most of which were not listed in my book anyway. I truly regretted that I had nothing more to offer them in in Yiddish.

Before the service began, I was handed a Sabbath *sider*; when I opened it, I saw an inscription that read "To Our Brethren in Lithuania from Your Brethren in Montreal." I sighed, remembering that my father had his *bar mitzvah* in Montreal in 1920. I easily followed the Hebrew service; when it concluded, several men wished me *"gut Shabes."* One man grasped my hand and wished me well, saying *"zayt gezunt."*

During the ensuing years, I occasionally took a night course in basic Yiddish, and even acquired lessons in books, on tapes and CDs. However, I never quite succeeded in getting beyond a phrase or two.

In 2000, I became involved with the Silicon Valley Holocaust Survivors Association in San Jose, California, and also began teaching a course at San Jose State University about how the American media covered the Holocaust during World War II. I became friends with many survivors and became closer to those who spoke Yiddish.

I could still only greet them with *"vos makhstu?"* and say good-bye with *"zayt gezunt."*

I have learned more phrases and some basic Yiddish grammar. I own more than two dozen dictionaries and books on the language and culture, including Uriel Weinreich's 790-page *Modern English-Yiddish, Yiddish-English Dictionary.*

I subscribe to *Der Bay,* a monthly publication written primarily in English, and follow its transliterated Yiddish writings. I take online Yiddish lessons from the Yiddish Book Center in Amherst, Massachusetts, and have been a member for years. I attend events listed on KlezCalifornia's site, and look forward to attending their Northern California Yiddish Culture Festival every spring. If a course in Yiddish is offered locally, I will try to attend.

All this is just a start, and I hope to go further. I hope the thirty-six expressions in *The Oy Way* are a starting point for you to learn more about a magnificent language and its rich history and culture.

Zayt gezunt!

glossary

alts	all
beygn	bent
bime	pulpit
bisl	bit
bupkus	nothing
chutzpah	nerve
davnen	pray
farshteyn	understand
gelt	money, funds
heymish	cozy
gut Shabes	good Sabbath
kop	head
kvetching	complaining
lerer	teacher
lernen	learn
mazl	luck
mekhaye	joy, delight, great pleasure
meshuge	crazy

pronunciation guide

The transliteration of Yiddish in this book follows the system of the YIVO Institute for Jewish Research, most readily used by the average reader of English.

The following guide will help you pronounce letters and combinations that may pose a question. The letters c, j, q, w and x are not used in Yiddish; other consonants are pronunced the same as in English.

a as in father

ay as in aye

dz as in amends

e as in set

ey as in they

g as in give

i as in sit

kh as ch in Bach

o as in core

ts as in lots

tsh as ch in chat

u as oo in book

zh as in Zhivago

starting stances

There are two basic starting stances for all the movements found in *The Oy Way*. Once you understand these stances and practice them, you will more easily begin each Oy Way movement.

The *shteyn* stance

To begin any movement that smoothly flows from the *shteyn* position, stand erect and place your feet facing directly forward, at the width of your shoulders. Inhale deeply through your nose, then exhale slowly through your mouth. Pause and feel the steadying connection with the surface beneath you. Slowly and rhythmically move your body up and down on your toes three times before settling down. You are now ready to begin any movement starting with the *shteyn*.

The *beygn* stance

To begin any movement that flows from the *beygn* position, place your feet at the width of your shoulders, facing outward at a slight angle, as shown in the photograph. Establish a solidly stabilized yet flexible foundation. Inhale deeply through your nose, then exhale slowly through your mouth. Slowly and rhythmically move your body up and down three times on your toes. Lower your behind a *bisl* into the *beygn* stance. You are now ready for any movement that begins with the *beygn*.

Master the stances, and the Oy Way movements await you

As with anything in life that you deem worthwhile attaining, practice these starting stances until you feel relaxed and comfortable with them. At that point you will be able to easily and successfully step into any of the Oy Way movements.

The author and friends perform the kum aher! *movement at Esalen, Big Sur, California*

questions

When you ask someone a question, you may receive a question in return. If its purpose is to gain further clarification, that is quite acceptable for purposes of successful communication. Such a response can also be used as a method of deflection or avoidance. If the response to "Understand me?" is "What do you mean by that?" then you have become involved in the back-and-forth game of interrogatory table tennis. To avoid such a potentially debilitating match, you should refrain from answering with "What do you think I mean?" Don't give up, though; you may find the answers in the expressions and movements in this chapter.

1

farshteyestu?

fahr-shtay-stew?

do you understand?

movement

Assume the *shteyn* stance.

Tighten your face muscles inward and present a sincerely quizzical look.

Stretch your head forward and stare straight in front of you.

Shrug your shoulders and thrust both arms forward waist-high with palms facing up.

Raise and lower your extended arms chest-high three times as you ask "*farshteyestu?*"

Return to your natural center.

benefits

By knowing what needs to be said and how to say it, the *farshteyestu?* movement can open doors to more meaningful communication.

❧ Helps reduce and possibly even eliminate facial wrinkles.

❧ Enables you to communicate successfully using only your upper body.

❧ Releases undue tension accumulated in your neck and shoulders.

thoughts

Once you head in a different direction from before, you open up to unknown possibilities.

While many try to age gracefully, there is really no reason to do so.

With the right effort, you can get others to listen to you; however, there is no guarantee they will understand what you are trying to say.

2
gib a kuk
gib a cook
give a look

movement

Assume the *shteyn* stance.

Take a deep breath and focus straight ahead.

Without turning your head, use your peripheral vision and notice an object or some person on your right.

Slowly and inconspicuously turn and face that object or person.

Raise your eyebrows, scrunch your nose, and stare intensely at that object or person. Raise your right arm, point your forefinger in that direction and enthusiastically chant *"gib a kuk."*

Lower your eyebrows, unscrunch your nose, and slowly return to the *shteyn* stance.

Repeat this movement by noticing an object or person on your left.

Return to calmness.

benefits

When you are into the *gib a kuk* movement, you become better able to see what lies ahead, and are less likely to be immersed in what happened in the past.

❧ You will gain the ability to face a hidden reality with neither fear nor trepidation.

❧ Your eyebrows will become more flexible and your *noz* may be less susceptible to congestion.

❧ You will be more conscious of your surroundings without having to exert untold effort.

4

thoughts

Too often in life you may not notice all that is beautiful just outside your vision's grasp.

You need to feel comfortable and to seek out what seems to be just beyond your realm.

With a minimum of effort, you are capable of discovering new worlds.

3
kum aher!
koom ah-hare!
come here!

movement

Assume the *beygn* stance.

Extend your right arm straight out in front of you with the palm of your right hand facing heaven.

Clench your right hand into a fist that faces toward your body and extend your forefinger upward.

Don't force the movement; offer a sincere, warm smile, and wiggle your forefinger strongly but unthreateningly three times toward your body as you say *"kum aher!"*

Return to the *beygn* stance and repeat the movement using your left arm.

benefits

With a grasp of what you need to do to make your world better, the *kum aher!* movement can more readily convince others that they too can be part of that world.

❦ Helps to bring others closer to you.

❦ Helps to bring you closer to others.

❦ Improves digital dexterity needed in a digital society.

thoughts

You can command attention from others by making the right moves.

To inspire others, you must first discover a profound reason to do so.

People can respond positively when the motivation seems solid and sincere.

4
vos makhstu?
vohs makh-stew?
how are you doing?

movement

Assume the *shteyn* stance.

Relax and give in to the flow as you extend your arms forward waist-high with your palms facing upward.

Breathe in and out deeply and sincerely.

Move your arms to your chest, then throw them forward, put a quizzical look on your face, and enthusiastically ask *"vos makhstu?"*

Return to the *shteyn* stance.

Repeat the movement, to show that you are truly interested in the other person.

benefits

When you use the *vos makhstu* movement and show others you are interested in their lives, they in turn may become more receptive to you and your life.

❧ Encourages deeper and healthier breathing.

❧ Invites friends in to enjoy and benefit from your positive attention to them.

❧ Opens your flow and gradually invites those you query into your life.

thoughts

Curiosity about others enhances their lives by providing them with a feeling of belonging.

We are all alone in the world; we have to learn to be alone together.

When you ask about the welfare of others, their response may help you find out more about yourself.

5

zog gornisht
sawg gore-nisht
keep quiet

movement

Assume the *beygn* stance.

Focus your attention straight ahead, scrunch your forehead and slightly raise your eyebrows.

Place your right forefinger to your lips and hold for a count of five.

Move that forefinger forward and backward five times, quietly repeating "*zog gornisht*" with each move.

Return to the *beygn* stance.

Repeat the movement using your left forefinger.

benefits

While speaking the truth when requested is a desirable trait, if you revert to the *zog gornisht* movement at times, you will discover silence can be golden.

❦ Provides you with the opportunity to successfully take charge of a possibly disturbing situation.

❦ Others may respect you even more so when you show timely leadership.

❦ You will increase your forefinger-to-lips dexterity.

thoughts

In our frenetic world, we are all responsible to help quiet things down.

Sometimes seemingly small actions inspire calmness and your mind can be set free.

It is not always necessary to raise your voice to get your thoughts and points across to others.

philosophy

When you speak Yiddish, others may get the impression that what is being said is based on deep-seated and ancient philosophical revelations. In reality, Yiddish is an ever-evolving language; although its roots are more than a thousand years old, a new philosophical meaning can be unveiled when minds are open to doing so. As the world rapidly changes, there may be something new under the sun waiting to be found. You only have to pause, search and discover what challenges may await you. If you can believe in yourself, there may be much more you can accomplish, but you won't know until you try. Just make the effort by trying this chapter's movements.

6
alts iz gut
ahlts is goot
everything is all right

movement

Assume the *shteyn* stance.

Don't force the movement; extend your right arm in front of you and raise it to chest height.

Move your right thumb to your right forefinger and create a circle.

Move your right hand forward and back three times, smile and say *"alts iz gut"* with each move.

Return to the *shteyn* stance and repeat the movement using your left arm and hand.

benefits

Even when you feel discombobulated and your world seems to have gone awry, the *alts iz gut* movement can help you see your world in a different light.

❡ Promotes both essential finger-thumb dexterity and digital coordination.

❡ Helps to communicate positive thoughts without having to put forth a lengthy explanation.

❡ Gives others insight into your outlook on life and living.

thoughts

When life events seem to be getting away from your control, it is an opportune time to appreciate all that is going well.

A small gesture can be the starting point for inspiring larger actions.

Regardless of the status of any situation, brightness overshadows darkness.

7
az got vil, shist a bezem
as got vil, shist a beh-zem
if God wills, even a broom could shoot

movement

Assume the *shteyn* stance.

Feel energy and strength rise from beneath as you raise your head to the heavens and move your arms overhead with your palms facing down.

Bring your hands down to your side, extend your left forearm out fully and make a fist.

Place your right arm by your right eye, as if you are pulling taut a bowstring.

Stretch your right arm further back, hold firmly for six seconds and say *"az got vil, shist a bezem"* and then release.

Repeat three times and return to the *shteyn* stance.

Do the same movement with your right forearm extended.

benefits

With a belief in your ability to achieve the impossible and faith in yourself, the *az got vil, shist a bezem* movement will help you take aim at what can be done.

❡ Releases tightened and stressed shoulder muscles.

❡ Allows you to go far beyond your own perceived physical limits.

❡ Helps you to align your sights on seemingly faraway goals.

❡ You will experience a new sense of physical and emotional relief.

thoughts

What may seem impossible to others, if you make the effort, you may be able to attain.

Through the use of visualization, imagination and dedication, much can be achieved.

You are confronted by many challenges in life, and if you believe in yourself, you can accomplish much more than you ever thought possible.

8

az me leygt arayn, nemt men aroys

ahz meh laygt ah-rhine, nemt men ah-royce

what you put in, you take out

movement

Assume the *beygn* stance.

Maintain an easy mind and body and place your left foot forward.

Raise both arms to shoulder height, turn your hands outward and push forward.

Turn your arms so that both palms are now facing upward, and lower your arms below your waist.

Extend your arms forward and with palms facing inward, bring your arms to your chest and philosophically chant "*az me leygt arayn, nemt men aroys.*"

Return to the *beygn* stance.

Repeat the movement with your right foot forward.

benefits

With a sincere desire to help make the world a better place without expecting anything in return, doing the *az me leygt arayn, nemt men aroys* movement may reward your altruistic actions.

❧ Enables you to learn how to give and take as your body adjusts to changes in the universe.

❧ Lets you coordinate your upper body actions while you loosen your torso.

❧ Provides you with an opportunity to bring the outside world into your life.

thoughts

At times you must reach out to others if you want them to reach out to you.

If you are not complacent, the right actions may help you gain insight into conflict resolution.

Even the seemingly most innocuous actions can be meaningful to others.

9
ver veyst?
ver vayst?
who knows?

movement

Assume the *shteyn* stance.

Move with a natural flow as you extend your arms in front of you with your palms facing upward.

Place a benign yet meaningful smile upon your face.

Tilt your head ever so gently to the left and move it down until it lightly touches your left shoulder.

Shrug both shoulders and smile knowingly.

Raise and lower your arms three times, then nod your head up and down three times and solemnly say *"ver veyst?"*

Return to the *shteyn* stance and repeat the movement on your right side.

benefits

You can never really know what awaits you, but by sincerely doing the *ver veyst?* movement, you have grown, by admitting that you don't fully understand the vagaries of life.

❧ Helps to relieve accumulated neck stress.

❧ Relaxes your shoulder muscles, which may have become overwrought with tension.

❧ Helps bring equilibrium and balance to your life.

❧ Affords you the opportunity to be yourself as you learn to accept the inevitable.

thoughts

At times you may be questioned by another person or yourself, when you are diligently studying a perplexing situation that seems beyond your comprehension.

You should realize that some things are impossible to fully comprehend, and be willing to admit it.

This is an important step in understanding yourself and your *raison d'être*.

It is far better to accept than to expect.

10
vos vet zayn, vet zayn!
voz vet zine, vet zine!
what will be, will be!

movement

Assume the *beygn* stance.

Extend your right arm, raise it and point to the heavens above.

Waggle your forefinger four times and, if the feeling arises, also wiggle it.

Shrug your shoulders and slowly rock your head back and forth in harmony with the wind.

If there is no wind, either imagine that there is one or turn on a fan, as you say with acceptance, *"vos vet zayn, vet zayn!"*

Come back to the *beygn* stance and repeat the movement by extending your left arm.

benefits

You can discover the essence of self-acceptance and of philosophical tranquility by cultivating the *vos vet zayn, vet zayn!* movement and reaping its benefits.

❦ Acknowledging that there may be a higher force in the universe helps you to ease inner tension caused by actions beyond your control.

❦ You may help alleviate possible suffering, through your acceptance of any situation.

❦ Allows you to enjoy and embrace the moment.

thoughts

Acceptance of reality, even when it seems unreal or surreal, is a sign of growing maturity.

Learning to adjust in life is an important step in finding inner peace.

When you admit that at times you have limited or no control of external events, you will also realize that you have complete control of your responses to them.

fray

For far too long, our country has been experiencing the off-key sounds of the "Battle Hymn of the Republicans and the Democrats." You can sit back and wonder why this battle continues, or you can do something about it and any other unwanted situation that personally affronts you. It's not that difficult to get involved; if you don't feel up to tackling an enormous challenge all at once, you can do so a *bisl* at a time. Although you may feel that you are experiencing a deluge of negativity, you have the power in your words and actions to deflect it. You will find a helping hand when you move your entire body and do the exercises that follow.

11
genug iz genug!
geh-noog is geh-noog!
enough is enough!

movement

Assume the *shteyn* stance.

Without malice aforethought, create a stern but non-threatening look upon your face.

With your arms hanging loosely by your side, let your left arm easily rise chest-high and turn your left palm outward.

Push your left arm forward three times; with each move gently but firmly chant *"genug iz genug!"*

Bring your left arm back to your side.

Repeat this comforting action using your right arm.

benefits

You can become more at peace with any reality that appears to be far-fetched when you immerse yourself in the *genug iz genug!* movement and accept life's limitations.

- ❦ You will not only learn to stretch your body beyond what you thought to be its previous limits, but will also be able to block negative intrusions from entering your aura.
- ❦ Your shoulders will more readily release tension caused by general and specific unwanted outside influences.
- ❦ You will learn more about yourself and what is and what is not acceptable to you.

thoughts

Consciously or unconsciously you may become aware that you have limits about what you will accept from others, and more importantly, what you will accept from yourself.

It is important to set boundaries, to recognize them, and to then keep within them.

When you are faced with a sense of overwhelming intrusions from the outside, look inside yourself for a solution.

Learn to successfully evade anxiety and turmoil.

12
makhn a tsimis
ma-khin ah tsi-mess
making molehills
into mountains

movement

Assume the *beygn* stance.

Extend both arms forward with your palms facing down.

Lower your arms to knee height and push downward three times.

Slowly raise both arms waist-high and breathe in deeply. Slowly raise them chest-high and breathe in deeply, then slowly raise them head-high and breathe in deeply.

Slowly raise your arms overhead, breathe in deeply and say *"makhn a tsimis."*

benefits

What may appear to be a deep-seated problem can grow into something beyond your control unless you use the lessons of the *makhn a tsimis* movement to bring you back to reality.

❡ Helps to lengthen and strengthen your torso.

❡ Enables you to loosen tense shoulder and arm muscles.

❡ Stimulates blood flow as it enhances your breathing.

thoughts

If you have the right mindset and act faithfully, you will know no limits.

You can rise to new heights with a slow and steady effort.

There is more around you than you imagined, if you are willing to open up to new ideas.

13

oykh mir a lebn?

oykh mere ah leh-ben?

this you call a living?

movement

Assume the *beygn* stance.

Slowly sink down a *bisl* and turn both arms and hands to face forward.

Reach into where your pockets would be and quickly lower your empty hands in frustration.

Lower your head and turn it first left and then right, while you sadly eye your empty hands.

Shake your head left and right as you inquire *"oykh mir a lebn?"*

Return to the *beygn* stance and sigh.

benefits

Life is a constant struggle to stay even. When you are not satisfied with what you have, the *oykh mir a lebn?* movement will help you realize that you can do something about it.

❧ By lowering your arms in despair, you are really reaching out for something better.

❧ May provide relief for a mild case of cervical spondylosis.

❧ If you are not wearing pants with pockets, or not wearing pants, this movement affords you a chance to utilize visualization abilities you may not realize you possessed.

thoughts

Do not be overwhelmed, for we must face the harsh reality of life and accept it.
   At times we must make an effort and take positive action.
   When things appear to be down, we may find an opportunity to rise up.

14
oy vey!
oi vay!
oh, woe!

movement

Assume the *shteyn* stance.

Be sure that your body is uncentered and that your mind is slightly cluttered.

Take a deep breath, tremble a bit at the knees, and let out a melancholy sigh.

Shrug your shoulders and hold for five seconds after you have gone as high as possible without leaving the ground. Release your shoulders.

Gently, but firmly, smack the left side of your head with the palm of your left hand, look upward and plaintively moan *"oy vey!"* Return to the *shteyn* stance.

Gently, but firmly, smack the right side of your head with the palm of your right hand, look upward and once again moan *"oy vey!"*

Repeat this movement five times, or until you have satisfactorily expressed your feelings, or your headache has become too severe to continue.

benefits

With a troubled mind, a strong head, and an unbending belief, the challenging *oy vey!* movement can take you to new levels.

❧ You will become more adept at expressing your innermost feelings.

❧ You will feel a greater blood flow to your brain, providing energy for untold mental challenges.

❧ Your palms will become fonts of strength.

❧ You will learn how to induce cranial pain, but you will feel much better after discontinuing this movement.

thoughts

Although you may actively seek life's pleasures, life's woes are apt to find you. Do not avoid the unavoidable. All is not lost when the pain of undeserved woe invades your sacred territory.

Even if you are unable to rid yourself of the negativity, by merely recognizing it, you are taking your first step toward inner peace on the Oy Way path.

It may not help the woe to be gone, but you may find a gentle way of easing the pain and negativity. Realize that it does exist, and know that only you can do something about it.

15
veyst fun bobkes
vayst foon bub-kiss
knows very little

movement

Assume the *beygn* stance.

Gently shake you head from side to side, slowly purse your lips and pout a bit.

Extend both arms in front of you waist-high, with your palms facing down.

Let your arms slowly and naturally glide up and down six times.

Drop your head to your chin and exude a benevolent expression of understanding by saying *"veyst fun bobkes."*

Bring your hands together in a praying position and gently return to the *beygn* stance.

benefits

If knowledge is power, then by judiciously using the *veyst fun bobkes* movement you will be able to discern how to best interrelate with others.

❧ Allows you to be a *bisl* judgmental about others and their knowledge of life, without being either too harsh or dogmatic.

❧ Provides you with the realization that you could be the other person one day.

❧ This movement enables you to quickly and surely express yourself in a kosher manner.

thoughts

It is a very wise person who knows that she or he knows very little.

This realization is the first step in understanding how much more you may need to learn.

The next step is to pursue, learn about and accumulate *seykhl*, which can only come by not trying to learn it.

descriptions

At times when you are faced with an inappropriate occurrence that is totally unacceptable, some people may judge you by observing your immediate reaction to the situation. However, it is equally important for you to recognize what your attitude was then and what it will be in the future. You are solely responsible for deciding what is and is not important in your life. You can accept the occurrence, or become even stronger by walking away. It is also up to you to follow through with these beneficial movements.

16
bisl meshuge
bisel meh-shoo-geh
a little bit crazy

movement

Assume the *beygn* stance.

Look straight ahead and visualize a being you have created—one whose actions may be a bit skewed from any accepted norm.

Move your right forefinger to your right ear.

Take a deep breath, exhale and twist your finger in a counterclockwise circle five times; each time, sympathetically say *"bisl meshuge."*

Return to the *beygn* stance and repeat the same action starting with your left forefinger and left ear.

benefits

Without a stable relationship with yourself, the *bisl mishuge* movement may enable you to recognize what it takes to foster a realization of your own true self.

❧ Helps increase hand-to-ear coordination while keeping your wrists flexible.

❧ Good for possibly helping to delay and even prevent arthritis.

❧ Improves digital dexterity, which will be needed if dial phones make a comeback.

❧ Brings a smile of acceptance and understanding to your *ponem*.

thoughts

With the knowledge that the world is overflowing with *narishkeyt*, this is a step forward to finding enduring inner peace.

Being able to determine who is propagating the *narishkeyt* helps you better understand others and their frailties.

By quietly and sympathetically noting those living in another world without exclaiming loudly, you may become more humane on your road to self-actualization.

17
a gantse megile
a gahn-tseh meh-gill-eh
big deal

movement

Assume the *beygn* stance.

Place your arms at the sides of your body, with each of your palms gently touching its corresponding leg.

Move your arms outward and up in a circular motion over your head until the fingers on both hands touch.

Vigorously throw your arms open three times and enthusiastically proclaim *"a gantse megile."*

Bring your arms down again, breathe deeply and pause for a count of four.

Find harmony as you enthusiastically repeat this invigorating action three more times.

benefits

It is imperative for you to be able to recognize what is important and what is not, and the *a gantse megile* movement can help you to accept whatever comes your way.

❦ Loosens tight shoulder muscles as it helps relieve tension.

❦ Enables your true spirit to flow freely.

❦ Helps to dissipate and remove evil dwelling within.

❦ Resting between movement segments affords you an opportunity to clear your mind.

thoughts

At times, when attempting to flow freely, it may seem more difficult than it really is. You will be able to if you are ready and willing to try.

To open your inner self to what has been bothering you becomes less of *a gantse megile* if you accept who you are without reservations.

Don't get trapped in the past.

18

in mitn derinen
in mitten der-in-en
in the middle of it all

movement

Assume the *shteyn* stance.

Extend both arms in front of you waist-high.

Move your elbows outward and create a circle by gently touching the fingertips of both hands together in front of you.

Breathe deeply and easily.

Open your circle, and as you bring your arms outward, separate your fingers and offer *"in mitn derinen."*

Hold this position for a count of six, and shrug your shoulders.

Repeat this invigorating movement five times.

Bring your arms in, place your hands on your belly and smile knowingly.

benefits

When you are surrounded by negativity and feel trapped, the *in mitn derinen* movement will help you realize how important it is to have a positive attitude.

❡ By reaching outward and then allowing the world back into your life, you can expand your horizons.

❡ You will be gathering in the life force known in the Yiddish world as *chai*.

❡ *Chai* will help you to grow and blossom.

thoughts

At times life moves outward from yourself; at other times you must accept an inward flow like ripples caused by a pebble gently dropped in the still waters of a small pond.

You can let yourself become more of a creator of energy with your actions when you reach out to others.

You may become more in harmony with the universe.

19
shtark vi ayzn
shtark vee eye-zen
strong like iron

movement

Assume the *shteyn* stance.

Raise your right arm to the side at shoulder level; take a deep breath and fully expand your chest.

Raise your right forearm and clench your fist.

Tighten and loosen your right biceps three times; with each motion smile knowingly and emphatically say *"shtark vi ayzn."*

Lower your right arm and settle back into the *shteyn* stance.

Repeat the movement using your left arm.

benefits

While outer strength may be a visible manifestation of devoted physical effort, you can develop important inner strength and resolve with the *shtark vi ayzn* movement.

❡ Releases inherent biceps tension in both arms.

❡ Makes others more aware of your inner strength and helps prevent confrontations.

❡ Provides you with more confidence in whatever you attempt to do.

thoughts

When people become aware of the hidden strengths of others, harmonious interaction may be increased.

It is never too late to develop muscles in your body and in your mind to earn the respect of others.

When others doubt our abilities and strengths, it is helpful to declare and modestly reveal them.

20
sheyn ponem
shayn puh-nem
pretty face

movement

Prelude: While this expression is usually said to a female, to avoid an unnecessary confrontation with her companion when you use the movement, it is safer to make yourself the recipient of the action.

Assume the *shteyn* stance.

Raise your right arm to your right cheek and gently grab the skin beneath your right cheekbone with your thumb and forefinger.

Squeeze firmly three times, and say *"sheyn ponem"* with each gentle and loving squeeze.

Sigh and smile as you return to the *shteyn* stance.

Repeat the movement using your left arm and hand.

benefits

Some go to extremes trying to paint an unnatural portrait of outward beauty, but it is far better to seek inner cerebral perfection by doing the *sheyn ponem* movement.

❧ Can help to put a healthy glow upon your face.

❧ May prevent arthritis in your thumbs and forefingers.

❧ Gives you an invigorating and stimulating tingle.

thoughts

We must all take responsibility for the results of our actions or inactions.

At times, performing small, simple actions can bring about untold results.

You don't have to wait for others when you are fully capable of initiating a positive effort.

prayer

You don't have to enter a *shul,* church, temple or mosque to pray for what you truly believe in, or for what you want. Whether you seek something as esoteric and meaningful as world peace, or just a little more *gelt* on payday, you can pray without entering a man-made structure. You can find solace walking through a meadow or a forest, by the calm waters of a still pond, or by the turbulent waters of an angry sea. You don't have to be angry, and at times secular prayer can be a blessing. With a little effort you can find something to believe in, and it will help to do the movements found in this chapter.

21
a brokh oyf dayn kop
ah brokh oyf dine cup
a blessing on your head

movement

Assume the *beygn* stance.

Imagine a child standing in front of you whose height just reaches your waist.

Tuck your hands together under your chin in a prayer pose, nod your head three times and smile broadly.

Let your left arm easily rise, and with the palm of your hand, softly pat the imaginary child on the head three times; each time you do so, gently say *"a brokh oyf dayn kop."*

Return to the *beygn* stance and offer an even broader smile.

Repeat the movement using your right arm and hand.

benefits

The *a brokh oyf dayn kop* movement will help you to not dwell in the past, to live fully in the present, and to accept what the future may have waiting for you.

❦ Stretches and loosens your facial muscles.

❦ Can help to reduce unwanted wrinkles. If you would rather look older, skip this movement.

❦ Affords you the possibility of extending arm length.

thoughts

Offers an opportunity to challenge yourself as you reach out to others.

The future belongs to the young, and it is a *mitsve* to inspire them.

No one stands taller than someone who reaches for another by making the effort of bending down.

22
keyn eyn hore
kane ane haw-reh
no evil eye

movement

Assume the *beygn* stance.

Place your hands on your chest, extend your arms as you push outward and look to the heavens. Bring your right arm back to your side.

Extend the palm of your left hand outward and move your right forefinger near your right eye; wiggle your finger three times, and with conviction say *"keyn eyn hore."*

Lower both hands and repeat the movement by extending the palm of your right hand, moving your left forefinger to your left eye, and wiggling it three times.

With your palms open and facing you, place your hands over your eyes, and rotate your head from side to side in a knowing "no" action of acute awareness.

benefits

By being open to the possibility of both the positive and negative aspects of the supernatural, you will be more aware of your choices when you engage in the *keyn eyn hore* movement.

❡ Allows you to escape from that which you may consciously
  or subconsciously fear.

❡ Helps you expand your breathing capacity.

Caution: Do not let your wiggling forefinger come too close to your eye; doing so could inadvertently result in a scratched cornea. If you have not yet mastered this form of digital dexterity, consult an ophthalmic surgeon before attempting this movement.

thoughts

In life, you may be confronted by evil, no matter how hard you try to avoid it.

The secret of confronting such unwanted situations is first being able to recognize them, then attempting to avoid them, and finally warding them off.

The popular *gay avek!* movement on page 64 may also help to deflect any negativity.

23
fun dayn moyl
in Gots oyern
foon dine moyl in Gots oyern
from your mouth to God's ears

movement

Assume the *shteyn* stance.

Open you mouth slightly and raise your right hand to cover your oral chasm.

Be still and look inside yourself as you gaze upward to the heavens (or your ceiling) and smile.

Slowly and sincerely raise your right arm above your head.

Lower your arm, cup your hand over your right ear, and in a deeply reverential voice say *"fun dayn moyl in Gots oyern."*

Return to the *shteyn* stance and repeat the movement on your left side.

benefits

A true believer begins her or his journey by seeking the truth from whatever sources are available, and the *fun dayn moyl in Gots oyern* movement can connect a person with an unexpected source.

❡ By reaching for new heights, you may raise yourself to a higher plain.

❡ When you search for something and are open to all sides, you may discover the truth.

❡ As it is written in Matthew 7:7, "Seek, and ye shall find." *Nu?* So don't hide, go seek.

thoughts

You can attain a higher level of spirituality by becoming more willing to express yourself.

It may take a lifelong quest to find the meaning of life, but you can only find it if you continue searching.

You may never know if anyone is listening to what you are saying, but keep on saying it, just in case they are.

24
hu ha!
hoo hah!
I am amazed!

movement

Assume the *beygn* stance.

Let your mind float freely and be receptive to all that the universe has to offer you.

Plant your right foot forward, and your left foot back.

Be centered and find tranquility in the moment. Your body is at ease, and you are ready to initiate the *hu ha!* movement.

Extend your right arm forward at shoulder height.

Make a gentle fist, and extend your forefinger forward.

Bend your arm at the elbow and point towards the heavens.

Raise your head upward, flick your forefinger up and down three times, while chanting *"hu ha!"* Hold the position for a count of five.

Repeat the movement with the left arm, hand, and forefinger.

For maximum benefit, repeat the complete set of movements seven times.

benefits

With a willingness to believe in that which is unexplainable, and a feeling that the Oy Way offers something for you, the *hu ha!* movement provides you with invigorating benefits.

❡ You will feel stress leave your neck and gently float away.

❡ Your forefinger dexterity will improve.

❡ You will help ward off digital arthritis.

❡ You will be connected with the heavens, and become more at one with the universe.

56

thoughts

At a time of discombobulation, you may feel like a stranger within your own universe. This will remain so if you are unaware of the beauty that surrounds you.

When you open your eyes, your heart, and your soul to the unlimited possibilities of discovery, life's beauty and richness will not pass you by.

By being aware, you will be amazed at what a surfeit of joys are nearby, as you connect with the earth and the heavens in childlike innocence.

25
iz makh nisht
keyn untersheyd
es mahkht nisht cane oonter-shade
it makes no difference

movement

Assume the *shteyn* stance.

Raise both your arms chest-high with the palms of your hands facing outward.

Slowly push forward three times, and each time strongly utter the words *"iz makh nisht keyn untersheyd."*

Return to the *shteyn* stance, take a deep breath and knowingly sigh.

Repeat the movement three more times.

benefits

On the one hand, you must remember there is always the other hand. If you seek to discover in which hand is hidden the true meaning of life, then the *iz makh nisht keyn untersheyd* movement can help you.

❡ Your wrists could become far more flexible.

❡ Such subtle movements could make you more supple.

❡ Extended arms can help release upper torso tensions.

thoughts

There is much that we initially believe to be of great importance, but in the end we discover that it doesn't really matter.

You must learn to discern what really has meaning in your life and sweep aside the extraneous.

Enjoy what you have and avoid seeking that which you don't really need.

admonitions

To find order, you may have to exert yourself vocally and let your true feelings be known to those who are not treating you in a righteous manner. What is most important is to realize that, although some may be going out of their way to burden you with unwanted *narishkeyt,* you have the right to deflect it. In fact you have a responsibility to do so, to maintain your own sanity and your own well-being. Your deflections can take place by letting others know what you truly feel, by moving away from a protagonist, or by performing the movements found in this chapter.

26
er redt narishkeyt
ehr red-et nahrish-kate
he talks nonsense

movement

Assume the *beygn* stance.

Raise your right arm to shoulder height and point an accusatory finger straight ahead at an imaginary person.

Move your hand to your lips, place your forefinger against your thumb, and open and close them five times while saying *"er redt narishkeyt."*

Return to the *beygn* stance, firmly plant your feet and repeat the movement on the left side.

benefits

When you are face to face with someone who inundates you with irritating babble, or you become the initiator of such, then the *er redt narishkeyt* movement helps you to both recognize this and to change.

❧ Helps increase your thumb-to-forefinger coordination.

❧ By extending both arms, you increase your ability to point things out to others.

❧ Can bring untold relief by loosening stiff neck muscles.

thoughts

All of us are inundated with *narishkeyt* and must learn to deflect it.

By becoming aware of that which is negative, you have a better opportunity to reject it.

When the unwanted invades your life, you have the ability to evade it.

27

gey avek!
gay ah-veck!
get out of here!

movement

Assume the *beygn* stance.

Center your body and your mind, by placing your left foot forward and your right foot back. Slowly close your eyes, take a deep breath, bend slightly at the knees, and let all thoughts flow freely.

Extend your arms forward at shoulder height. Bend your hands upward at the wrists with your palms facing forward. Stretch your arms out, and firmly whisper *"gey avek!"* Hold for a count of five.

Bring both hands back to your chest and place them together tucked beneath your chin in a prayer position. Hold for a count of five.

Push forward once again, and repeat this set seven times.

Each time, slowly raise the intensity of your *gey avek!* mantra.

This will help to ensure that your incantations are most effective, as you approach a meaningful, yet temporary, state of nirvana.

benefits

With a receptive mind, a willing body, and a fervent belief in the Oy Way, the effortless *gey avek!* movement offers you manifold benefits.

❧ You will become adroit at pushing negative thoughts and negative people safely out of reach.

❧ You will soon feel inner tension dissipate, as the movement helps you alleviate pent-up stress in your shoulders.

❧ Weak arm muscles become strengthened, enabling you to more easily handle small burdens.

❧ Your wrists become more supple and energized.

thoughts

Whenever you feel that some negative force in the universe is trespassing on your tranquility, it is intuitive, logical and necessary to get into the proper meditational mindset. You will be on your way to rid yourself of any disconcerting intrusion.

That intrusion could be a thought, another person, or a way of life that is hampering your well-being.

Be firm yet gentle in your approach, and soon calmness and serenity will once more surround you—or perhaps be with you for the first time.

28
gey shray gevald
gay shrigh geh-vald
go shout in protest

movement

Assume the *shteyn* stance.

Extend your arms as far out to the sides as possible with the palms of your hands facing up.

Move both hands to your lips and throw your arms outward with a grimace.

Open your mouth and enthusiastically shout *"gey shray gevald."*

Note: The audible level of your shout should be sympathetic to where the shouting is taking place.

It is not recommended to do so in a church, synagogue or mosque.

If you are unharmed after the movement, slowly return to the *shteyn* stance.

benefits

When you have something on your mind that is preventing you from moving forward, the *gey shray gevald* movement empowers you to become better able to release pent-up and unwanted tension.

❡ Helps you rid yourself of hidden anger toward others.

❡ Can aid in reducing pent-up arm and shoulder tension.

❡ May help clear deeply encrusted throat problems.

thoughts

Resist the impulse to let anger envelop you by finding a way to harmlessly release it.

There is a plethora of ways to reduce tension—select whatever fits your lifestyle.

Outside influences can overwhelm you, but only if you let them do so.

29
loz em geyn
lawz im gain
let me be

movement

Assume the *shteyn* stance.

Place both hands in front of you waist-high, with the tips of your fingers barely touching.

Lower your left arm to your side.

Raise your right arm and extend it forward with your palm facing outward. Hold for a count of six.

Drop your arm, stand erect and nod your head up and down three times as you plaintively plead *"loz em geyn."*

Return to the *shteyn* stance and repeat the movement starting with your left arm.

benefits

When a feeling of being enclosed pervades your life and you seek freedom, the *loz em geyn* movement offers you an opportunity to release your feelings and set you free.

❡ These gentle actions will afford you both physical and mental relaxation.

❡ You will feel an illuminating breeze cool your body and caress your mind.

❡ You will gain new self-respect, and increase the possibility of garnering greater respect from others.

❡ You have quietly requested to be left alone, which is your inherent right.

thoughts

At times, the only way you can find true peace is to express your wishes to those who may be continually entering your space uninvited.

Let your bonds loosen, for it is neither rude or abrupt to let others know to what extent they can enter your space.

If you let others decide for you, then you are negligent in treating yourself to what you deserve.

30
zitsn oyf shpilkes
zit-sen oyf shpill-kehs
sitting on pins and needles

movement

Assume the *beygn* stance.

Lower your *tush* into a crouching position, so you are almost sitting while standing.

Shake your entire body, either to and fro or hither and yon.

Slowly transition into a *shteyn* stance by fully standing up. Move back into the *beygn* stance, then up to the *shteyn* stance, each time saying *"zitsn oyf shpilkes."*

Take a deep breath and sigh.

benefits

You may take intense situations for granted until you are willing to recognize them, face them head-on, and conquer them, by doing the *zitsn oyf shpilkes* movement.

❦ Releases all tensions confined to your lower torso.

❦ Can help alleviate and relieve constipation problems.

❦ Offers you an opportunity to make your entire body more flexible.

thoughts

When you feel the pressure of planning and initiating significant events, know that you have a modicum of control over your attitude toward them.

Physically and psychologically moving away from your troubles is a sign of maturity.

To maintain mental integrity, there are times when it is best to immediately face an unenviable situation.

nirvana

You can gain a modicum of spiritual enlightenment and attain a feeling of liberation by accepting what is, then moving on. You possess the power to free yourself from what is holding you back. When you do, you can accomplish more than what you thought to be possible. However, you are the one person responsible for finding answers to questions you didn't even ask. When you do, offer yourself positive reinforcement and congratulate yourself for the effort. When you look at life and living, standing in a positive posture, you are more than ready to accept and use the movements that follow in a beneficial manner.

31
halevay
hah-leh-vigh
I wish it so

movement

Assume the *shteyn* stance.

Raise your left hand upward, close your eyes and squeeze them tightly shut. Hold for a count of six as you breathe deeply.

Place your hands together, raise them to your chin, look to the heavens, smile, sigh, and softly say *"halevay."*

Gently rock your body back and forth and return to your center of calmness.

Repeat the movement by raising your right hand upward.

benefits

If you have an open mind and a willingness to forge ahead, your dreams can become realities when you exert a meaningful effort, using the *halevay* movement as a stepping stone.

❧ Helps relieve unwanted stress in your upper neck.

❧ Provides insight into the meaning of nirvana.

❧ Loosens your back as it frees you from self-imposed constraints.

❧ Affords you an opportunity for inspirational, ecumenical prayer.

thoughts

You sometimes need faith to help sustain you in your daily life.

Conversely, regardless of your religious affiliation or non-affiliation, it's good to have a belief in something other than yourself, along with believing in yourself.

As Ilene Woods sang in the title role of Disney's *Cinderella*, "A dream is a wish your heart makes."

32

nisht geferlekh
nisht geh-fair-lekh
no big deal

movement

Assume the *shteyn* stance.

Turn your arms forward with open palms and shrug your shoulders.

Squeeze tightly for a count of four.

Tilt your head to the left, stretch your neck and wrinkle your brow as you say *"nisht geferlekh."*

Release your brow and return to the *shteyn* stance.

Repeat the movement and tilt your head to the right.

benefits

By taking advantage of the *nisht geferlekh* movement no matter what the circumstances may be, it will help you to integrate a willingness to accept the extremes in life with a *laissez-faire* attitude.

❧ Releases endorphins and stimulates thinking.

❧ Eases mental stress, when you realize that what is, is.

❧ Opens up possibilities for gentler times ahead.

thoughts

With anything that happens, try to refuse and diffuse its negative aspects.

By accepting the extremes and reacting to them with an even temperament, you may find calmness and tranquility.

When you hear the sound of hoofbeats, don't look for zebras.

33
nu?
noo?
so?

movement

Assume the *shteyn* stance.

Shrug your shoulders straight up and hold for five seconds.

With your elbows by your side and your palms facing up, raise your arms to waist height.

Drop and raise your arms three times and sympathetically ask with each move *"nu?"*

Diligently repeat this movement five times.

Return to the *shteyn* stance and relax.

benefits

You will be better prepared to face adversity if you immerse yourself in the *nu?* movement whenever it is needed.

¶ Helps to possibly extend your body length, without shortening it.

¶ Can contribute to your lightness of being.

¶ May strengthen your resolve.

thoughts

You will never know what's new unless you ask about it.

An inquiring mind will help you find answers to questions you did not even ask.

Exploring the unexplored can be an exhilarating experience if you allow yourself to embrace it.

34
ot azoy!
awt ah-zoy
way to go!

movement

Assume the *beygn* stance.

Extend your left arm in front of you waist-high and clench your left hand into a fist of approval, not of defiance.

Smile as you raise and lower your left arm three times from your elbow.

Thrust your head forward in a gesture of approval as you raise your voice and happily exclaim *"ot azoy!"* with each thrust.

Lower your left arm and relax in the *beygn* stance.

With boundless energy, repeat the movement with your right arm and hand.

benefits

When you take the time to weigh out the positive and negative aspects of your life, the positive will have a better opportunity to prevail if you use the *ot azoy!* movement.

❦ Strengthens your hand muscles as it strengthens your resolve.

❦ Helps you learn to confront the uncomfortable with ease.

❦ Enables you to not only laud others but also to deservedly praise yourself.

thoughts

Life offers you countless opportunities and directions to take if you open the door to them.

Once you have been made aware of these, it is up to you to act; in doing so, you may achieve more than you ever imagined.

It is important to allow yourself to be yourself, and to congratulate yourself for your achievements whether they are large or small.

35

zolst lebn un zayn gezunt

zawlst leh-ben un zine geh-zunt

you should live and be well

movement

Assume the *beygn* stance.

Smile effusively and knowingly as you raise your arms above your head to the heavens with your palms open and facing you.

Stretch your arms upward five times.

Gently rock your head up and down three times in a nirvana-inducing manner as you sincerely offer *"zolst lebn un zayn gezunt."*

Return to the *beygn* stance, expand your smile, and be at ease with the world and yourself.

benefits

If you have a positive feeling about yourself and your situation, when you integrate the *zolst lebn un zayn gezunt* movement into your life, you will be taking a huge step into inculcating this feeling into others.

❧ By smiling effusively, you help release endorphins, which helps to increase tranquility.

❧ As you gently rock your *kop*, you relax tightened neck muscles and encourage a heightened feeling of well-being.

❧ When you rock your entire body to and fro, and even hither and yon, you become one with your own true self.

thoughts

When you wish the best for others, your kind words may have a profound karmatic affect on yourself.

This "kosher karma" can reverberate and come back to you tenfold, like the return of a boomerang.

Although you might not be immediately rewarded for your kindness, be content knowing that you tried to bring peace into the universe, which can be its own reward.

end

Whether an ending is exceedingly positive or fraught with anguish, you can then move forward and attempt something new and challenging. What you decide to do next is within your control, but also could be out of your hands. You can choose the direction you wish to take and even select what paths you want to take. However, you never know what may occur along the way. Go with the flow into the final, meaningful movement.

36
dos iz alts
dus iz alts
that's all there is

movement

Assume the *shteyn* stance.

Raise your arms to chest level and then bring both hands together just above your belly.

Slowly extend both your arms outward with your palms facing up, sigh happily or regretfully, depending on your frame of mind. Lift your arms three times saying *"dos iz alts."*

Knowingly sigh again and return to the *shteyn* stance.

benefits

With the knowledge that all things have a beginning and an ending, the *dos iz alts* movement reinforces what life is all about without having to make any judgments.

₵ Movements help to keep you limber and aware.

₵ Helps to keep your much-neglected palms feel they are part of your body.

₵ Your deep sighs help to facilitate a better flow of breath.

thoughts

All good things come to an end, but do not be sad, for if you loosen all bonds, with each ending there is potential for a unique new beginning.

All bad things also eventually come to an end; when they do, heartily rejoice.

Life is a mixture of good and bad; by meeting each instance with a degree of equanimity, you will find the sought-after necessary balance.

bibliography

dictionaries

Coldoff, Harry, *A Yiddish Dictionary in Transliteration.*
Proclaim Publications, 1988.

Galvin, Herman and Stan Tamarkin, *The Yiddish Dictionary Sourcebook.*
Ktav Publishing, 1986.

Gross, David C., *Yiddish Practical Dictionary.* Hippocrene Books, 2007.

Kogos, Fred, *A Dictionary of Yiddish Slang & Idioms.* Citadel Press, 2000.

———, *The Dictionary of Popular Yiddish Words, Phrases, and Proverbs.*
Citadel Press, 2005.

Weinreich, Uriel, *Modern English-Yiddish, Yiddish-English Dictionary.*
Schocken Books, 1977.

language

Ayalti, Hanan J., ed., *Yiddish Proverbs.* Schocken Books, 1976.

Kogos, Fred, *From Shmear to Eternity: The Only Book of Yiddish You'll Ever Need.*
Citadel Press, 2006.

Kumove, Shirley, *Words Like Arrows: A Treasury of Yiddish Folk Sayings.*
Warner Books, 1986.

———, *More Words, More Arrows: A Further Collection of Yiddish Folk Sayings.*
Wayne State University Press, 1999.

Rosten, Leo, *Hooray for Yiddish.* Touchstone, 1982.

———, *The New Joys of Yiddish.* Three Rivers Press, 2003.

history and culture

Karlen, Neal, *The Story of Yiddish: How a Mish-Mosh of Languages Saved the Jews.*
William Morrow, 2008.

Katz, Dovid, *Words on Fire: The Unfinished Story of Yiddish.* Basic Books, 2004.

Kriwaczek, Paul, *Yiddish Civilisation: The Rise and Fall of a Forgotten Nation.*
Vintage Books, 2006.

Lansky, Aaron, *Outwitting History: The Amazing Adventures of a Man Who Rescued
a Million Yiddish Books.* Algonquin Books, 2004.

Pekar, Harvey and Paul Buhle, eds., *Yiddishkeit: Jewish Vernacular & the New Land.*
Abrams ComicArts, 2011.

Samuel, Maurice, *In Praise of Yiddish*. Cowles Book Company, 1971.

Shepard, Richard F. and Vicki Gold Levi, *Live & Be Well: A Celebration of Yiddish Culture in America*. Rutgers University Press, 2000.

Steinmetz, Sol, *Yiddish and English: The Story of Yiddish in America*. University of Alabama Press, 2001.

Weinstein, Miriam, *Yiddish: A Nation of Words*. Steerforth Press, 2001.

Wex, Michael, *Born to Kvetch: Yiddish Language and Culture in All of Its Moods*. St. Martin's Press, 2005.

——, *Just Say Nu: Yiddish for Every Occasion (When English Just Won't Do)*. St. Martin's Press, 2007.

instruction

Mark, Yudel, *Invitation to Yiddish*. American Jewish Congress, with tape, 1982.

Zuckerman, Marvin and Marion Herbst, *Learning Yiddish in Easy Stages*. National Yiddish Book Center, with CD and test, 2000.

literature

Aleichem, Sholom, *Stories and Satires*. Collier Books, 1959.

——, *Favorite Tales of Sholom Aleichem*. Avenel, 1983.

Howe, Irving and Eliezer Greenberg, eds., *Voices from the Yiddish*. Schocken Books, 1975.

humor

Epstein, Lita, *If You Can't Say Anything Nice, Say It in Yiddish*. Citadel Press, 2006.

Small, Albert, ed., *A Treasury of Yiddish-American Cartoon Humor*. Companion Publications, 1998.

about the author

Harvey Gotliffe is the editor and publisher of *The Ho-Ho-Kus Cogitator* and its blog. He is a regular contributor to the *Huffington Post,* where he has written articles about Yiddish language and culture.

He has worked with Holocaust survivors since 2000, and written profiles of them in major print and online publications. In 2011, he was a presenter at the International Association of Yiddish Clubs Annual Conference talking about Yiddish-speaking survivors, and introduced *The Oy Way.*

Gotliffe has researched and written about the advertising of Holocaust denial in university newspapers, and made presentations in the United States and Israel. His research is archived at the United States Holocaust Memorial Museum.

In the second edition of the *Encyclopaedia Judaica* (2006), Gotliffe wrote the three-page article on the history of "The Jewish Press in America."

He has been a freelance writer since 1963, and in 1986 he founded and directed the award-winning magazine journalism program at San Jose State University; he retired in 2008.

Gotliffe has an MS in mass communications from San Jose State University and a PhD in radio, television and film from Wayne State University in Detroit. He lived in Israel in 1975 and 1976, where he conducted research for his doctoral dissertation: *Israeli General Television: A Historical Exploration of Content and Influence 1968–1973.*

Made in the USA
Charleston, SC
10 February 2012